THE FLORIDA PANTHER

Alvin and Virginia Silverstein
and Laura Silverstein Nunn

THE MILLBROOK PRESS BROOKFIELD, CONNECTICUT

The authors would like to thank Ken Alvarez, Robert Baudy, Chris Belden, Andy Eller, Judy Hancock, Brian Hunt, Dennis Jordan, Darrell Land, Tom Logan, Sidney Maddock, Dave Maehr, and Steve Williams, who generously shared their knowledge and insights and patiently answered our endless questions. Special thanks to Deborah Jansen, Dennis Jordan, and Steve Williams for their careful reading of the manuscript and their many helpful comments.

Cover photograph courtesy and © Tom & Pat Leeson, The National Audubon Society Collection/Photo Researchers Photographs courtesy and © Tom & Pat Leeson, The National Audubon Society Collection/Photo Researchers: p. 4; Florida Game & Freshwater Fish Commission: p. 7, 24 (R. Chris Belden), 33 (R. Chris Belden), 37; Animals, Animals: pp. 12 (© John Pointer), 15 (© John L. Pointer), 22 (© Maresa Pryor); Photo Researchers: pp. 18 (© David & Hayes Norris), 57 (© Tom & Pat Leeson); Orlando Sentinel: p. 40 (Joann Vitelli); Big Cypress National Preserve: p. 43 (Deborah Jansen)

Library of Congress Cataloging-in-Publication Data
Silverstein, Alvin.
The Florida panther / Alvin and Virginia Silverstein and Laura Silverstein Nunn.
p. cm. — (Endangered in America)
Includes bibliographical references (p.   ) and index.
Summary: Describes the physical characteristics, behavior, and habitat of the Florida panther as well as the efforts being made to save it from extinction.
ISBN 0-7613-0049-X (lib. bdg.)
1. Florida panther—Juvenile literature. 2. Endangered species—Florida—Juvenile literature. [1. Florida panther. 2. Pumas. 3. Endangered species.] I. Silverstein, Virginia B. II. Nunn, Laura Silverstein. III. Title. IV. Series: Silverstein, Alvin. Endangered in America.
QL737.C23S55 1997 599.74'428—dc20 96-42690 CIP AC

Published by The Millbrook Press, Inc.
2 Old New Milford Road Brookfield, Connecticut 06804

CONTENTS

The Wild Cats
5

The Florida Panther
9

A Florida Panther's Life
17

On the Brink of Extinction
23

Saving the Florida Panther
30

Future of the Florida Panther
44

Fingertip Facts **57**

Further Reading **59**

Organizations **61**

Index **63**

The Florida panther.

THE WILD CATS

In 1982, Florida schoolchildren chose the panther as their state animal. Today the license plates on many cars driven by Florida residents proudly display the panther's picture.

These large, tawny-colored cats did not always inspire such positive feelings, however.

The early settlers of the southeastern United States feared the panthers, believing that the animals were ferocious and dangerous to humans. The panther's secretive nature has led to unrealistic fears, myths, and misconceptions about it.

The Florida panther is more likely to avoid humans than to attack them. There are no documented reports of a Florida panther attacking a human. But the panther's imagined bad reputation has made it an easy target for humans, and human activities have played an important role in the rapid decline in the number of Florida panthers in the wild.

THE MISTAKEN ENEMY

Long before Columbus discovered America in 1492, Florida panthers were thriving throughout what is now the southeastern United States. The decline of the Florida panther population began in 1539, when Florida was discovered by Hernando de Soto, a Spanish explorer. As European settlers moved in, the wilderness areas where panthers could live shrank in size. The settlers not only took over panther territory; they actively attempted to get rid of these animals. They blamed the deaths of their livestock on the panthers, and because these wild cats seemed similar to African lions, the settlers feared for their own lives, too.

In 1832 a law was passed in the Territory of Florida that rewarded people for killing panthers. The law stated that a bounty, or reward, would be paid by the county courts. Florida became a state in 1845. In 1887 another bounty law was passed, authorizing a payment of five dollars (a lot of money then) for panther scalps in the State of Florida. The panthers that escaped being killed had to compete with hunters for deer, which was the panthers' favorite food.

In the late 1930s, people began hunting deer for other reasons, too. Deer carried ticks that could spread cattle fever, a deadly livestock disease. To save their cattle, the hunters wiped out nearly all the deer in southern Florida. The panthers were forced to stray from their home territories in search of food. Many panthers traveled into dangerous areas where they were killed by cars on highways or by ranchers protecting their livestock. Because of all these factors, the Florida panther is dangerously close to extinction.

BELATED CONCERN

As the population of Florida panthers dwindled, people began to realize that this native animal might be in danger of disappearing forever. Laws and regulations were soon established to protect the Florida panther. In 1950 the Florida panther was recognized as a game animal, and could be hunted only during the open season for hunting deer. If panthers destroyed livestock, however, landowners could get a special permit to kill them at any time. In 1958 the Florida panther was declared an endangered species and given complete legal protection by the Florida Game and Fresh Water Fish Commission.

Many Florida residents have special license plates like this one, declaring their support for the panther.

In 1967 the federal government officially put the Florida panther on the endangered species list. In 1973 the Endangered Species Act was passed and provided funds to bring the threatened animals back from the brink of extinction. In 1979, Florida state law made it a felony to kill a panther, with a penalty of five years in prison.

Unfortunately, laws that prohibited hunting did not solve the problem. Eventually, people realized that hunting was only one of the threats to the panthers' survival. As more people moved into panther territory and developed buildings and roads, the panthers were left with barely enough food and living space to survive.

Although the Florida panther had been recognized as an endangered species since 1967, the federal government had done little to help preserve it. It was not until 1976 that the species was given the attention it deserved. In March 1976 the Audubon Society sponsored a conference on the Florida panther, held in Orlando, Florida. It became clear that no one really knew much about the panther, or even if it still existed. As a result, a few months later, a Recovery Team was appointed by the U.S. Fish and Wildlife Service, and people were assigned to do field studies and search for any animals they could find in order to learn more about them.

Since then, scientists have learned much about these animals and their habitat. State wildlife biologists capture the panthers and attach collars with special radio devices to allow the animals' movements to be tracked. Various programs have been created to help save the Florida panther from extinction. Some scientists have considered breeding captive panthers to produce more of the animals, but breeding alone will not solve the problem. There must also be suitable places for the panthers to live, where they will find enough prey and will not interact with humans. Conservation plans must also include setting aside land for the Florida panther so that it will have a chance for survival.

THE FLORIDA PANTHER

Before Europeans settled in the New World, Florida panthers lived throughout the southeastern part of North America—from Arkansas to South Carolina to the tip of Florida. Now, the Florida panther, as its name suggests, is found only in southern Florida, primarily in the areas of Big Cypress and the Everglades.

THE CAT FAMILY

The Florida panther belongs to the cat family, *Felidae.* Scientists divide the cat family into the Big Cats and the Small Cats. The Big Cats, which include lions, tigers, leopards, and jaguars, are large, can roar, and have eyes with round pupils. The Small Cats, which include domestic cats, bobcats, and some other small species, typically are small, can purr, and have large eyes with oval pupils that contract into a vertical slit when exposed to bright light.

The Florida panther does not fit well into either of these categories. Like a Big Cat, it is large—a little larger than a leopard and nearly as large as a jaguar—and its pupils are round. But the Florida Panther purrs; it does not roar, although it can let out a bloodcurdling scream, similar to the yowling of housecats out on the prowl at night, but much louder. The panther's short, broad skull, rather small in proportion to the rest of its body, is also much more like the skulls of the Small Cats.

Despite its name, the Florida panther is not closely related to the panthers (also known as leopards) commonly found in southern Asia and Africa. It is actually a type of cougar, or mountain lion, whose scientific name is *Felis concolor,* which is Latin for "cat of one color." In 1896 a scientist, Charles B. Cory, first described the Florida panther as a subspecies of the mountain lion. In 1899, Outram Bangs, another scientist, gave the Florida panther its scientific name: *Felis concolor coryi,* in honor of its discoverer.

The cougar goes by many different names: mountain lion, panther, puma, catamount, and painter. It is more widely distributed than any other mammal in the Western Hemisphere, ranging from Alaska to Patagonia and from the shores of the Atlantic Ocean to the Pacific. The cougars that lived in different regions gradually adapted to the conditions of their homelands and developed differences in their body size and bone structure. Scientists have divided cougars into as many as thirty subspecies on the basis of these differences, but the cats themselves do not pay attention to such distinctions. Members of the different subspecies breed freely with each other. Florida panthers and Texas cougars *(Felis concolor stanleyana),* for example, once roamed some of the same lands and bred with each other until their populations were separated by human civilization. The Florida panther also bred with the eastern cougar *(Felis concolor cougar),* which became extinct in 1908, and the

Rocky Mountain cougar (*Felis concolor hippolestes*). Cougars are found in many western states, but Florida panthers are the only cougars known to live east of the Mississippi River.

WHAT DOES THE FLORIDA PANTHER LOOK LIKE?

Florida panthers are large cats with long tails and slender bodies. Adult males typically grow to about 7 feet (2 meters) from nose to tip of tail, and weigh an average of 120 pounds (55 kilograms). Female panthers weigh an average of only 80 pounds (36 kilograms) and grow to a length of about 6 feet (1.8 meters) or less. The panther is more than ten times the size of a house cat.

The Florida panther has shorter, stiffer hair than its western relatives. Its fur is yellowish brown along the back. The lower chest, belly, and inner legs are lighter in color. The tip of the tail, back of the ears, and parts of the face are highlighted with dark brown or black. Florida panther kittens are born with spots, but these markings disappear completely by the time the cats are two years old.

The color of the panther's coat serves a purpose for both kittens and adults. The spotted coloration of the kittens' fur blends into their surroundings and keeps them hidden in their den, safe from predators such as coyotes, alligators, and even adult male panthers. The coloring of the adults provides camouflage when they are hunting deer, their main prey. The adult panther's coat often matches the color of the deer.

A Cougar in Disguise

THE FLORIDA PANTHER is a distinctive type of cougar. The panther has a darker coat, longer legs, smaller feet, and is lighter in weight than any other cougar subspecies.

Many Florida panthers are distinguished by several unusual traits, including a whorl of hair (a cowlick) in the middle of the back; flecks of white fur around the head and shoulders; and a right-angle bend at the end of the tail. The cowlick and kinked tail are hereditary traits, but the white flecks are due to tick bites.

Panther kittens have spotted fur, which provides camouflage that keeps them safe from predators.

BUILT TO HUNT

The Florida panther is a large carnivore that requires substantial amounts of food. It often catches prey that is bigger than itself. White-tailed deer and wild hogs typically make up 75 percent of the panther's diet. A healthy panther usually kills a hog or deer every seven to ten days, and it may eat 20 to 30 pounds (9 to 14 kilograms) of meat in a single feeding. Although panthers prefer deer and hogs, they have been known to eat raccoons, armadillos, rabbits, cotton rats, birds, alligators, and even insects.

The physical features of the Florida panther reflect its predatory lifestyle. The panther's powerful jaws and teeth and its heavy bone structure allow it to overpower large prey. The surface of the tongue is studded with tiny sharp, horny points that are used to tear the meat from the bone. The panther has sensitive motion-detecting whiskers on its cheeks, upper lip, and above the eyelids.

The panther can move fast as it chases and captures its prey. A Florida panther can chase its prey at high speeds, sprinting as fast as 35 miles (56 kilometers) per hour—but only for short distances of about 200 yards (183 meters). The panther walks on its toes, with the back part of the foot raised. Webbed skin and fur between its toes muffle sound as the panther walks. Like a house cat, the panther can retract its claws, drawing them inward so they are completely covered. It usually walks with its claws retracted, but when it is ready to attack it extends its claws to seize its prey.

The Florida panther's large eyes and large pupils are well adapted for nighttime hunting. A reflecting layer at the back of the eyeballs helps to magnify even the faintest starlight or moonlight, providing a clear view of the panther's surroundings. During the day, the panther's pupils contract so that its eyes can adjust to the bright light. Unlike most cats, however, the Florida panther's pupils remain round rather than forming a slit when exposed to light. The animal's eyes are in the front of its head. The eyes work together to provide a good sense of depth and distance, which is important for an animal that chases and pounces on its prey. The panther is good at detecting movements, even at the corners of its eyes, but it has trouble noticing objects that are not moving. Deer and other prey sometimes "freeze" in place, remaining motionless to take advantage of the panther's shortcoming.

A panther's hearing is so sharp that it can pick up ultrasonic frequencies—sounds that humans cannot hear. Its ears move in the direction that the sound is coming from, acting as antennas to gather and magnify the sound. Panthers also have a very keen sense of smell and can track down prey by following their scent trails.

Florida panthers are most active at dawn and dusk. They spend the daytime resting. In southern Florida, panthers live in upland habitats, such as hardwood hammocks (high areas with rich soil and thick, junglelike forests), pine-palmetto forests, and cabbage-palm forests. During the day, they seek resting places in the dry uplands, which provide ample shade and seclusion. Panthers also spend a lot of time in wetland habitats (hardwood swamps, cypress swamps, freshwater marshes, and thicket swamps), even though they are not really swamp animals. In fact, these cats actually dislike swamplands, but because there has been little disturbance by human activities, prey is often plentiful there. Panthers also hunt around areas that were recently burned by fires because deer are attracted to the new plant life that springs up after a fire.

Once a Florida panther has tracked down its prey, it stalks the target carefully and quietly, waiting and watching for hours if nec-

A panther's body structure, tongue, teeth, eyesight, and hearing make the
animal an effective hunter.

Telltale Footprints

A FLORIDA PANTHER'S footprints are similar to those of a large dog. The imprints of both animals have four toes and a three-lobed pad that cushions the bottom of the foot. There is an easy way to tell the footprints apart. A dog's prints usually show the mark of a claw at the end of each toe. A panther walks with its claws retracted and does not leave claw marks.

---

essary. When the panther is ready to attack, it can pounce on a victim as far as 15 feet (4.6 meters) away.

HAVE YOU SEEN A FLORIDA PANTHER?

It is not easy to spot a Florida panther because there are so few of them, but many people claim to have seen one. People often mistake other animals, such as bobcats, house cats, or even dogs, for Florida panthers. The bobcat is spotted, much smaller, and has a shorter tail than the Florida panther. Feral cats (house cats returned to the wild) are also much smaller than the Florida panther. Because they are so similar, dog tracks can be mistaken for panther tracks. If you think you have seen a Florida panther, take a photograph of the animal or its tracks and give it to a wildlife agency to make an accurate identification.

A FLORIDA PANTHER'S LIFE

Florida panthers are usually solitary animals. Adult panthers try to remain isolated from each other and maintain their own large, well-defined territories or home ranges in which they live, hunt, and raise their young. Adult male panthers rarely share the home ranges of other males, but may share those of females, especially during the breeding season. Adult female panthers seem to be more tolerant of each other and often share the home ranges of other females.

The home ranges of male panthers are usually larger than those of females. Male panthers typically travel through a home range of 150 to 250 square miles (388 to 648 square kilometers), although some will cover 400 square miles (1,036 square kilometers) in search of prey. Female panthers usually have a home range of 70 to 90 square miles (180 to 233 square kilometers). A female's home territory is smallest when she has just given birth, but as the kittens grow, she has to travel farther to find food for them.

A Florida panther's territory is essential for its survival. Because individual territories are spread over great distances, confrontations between adult panthers are less likely. Panthers also hunt more efficiently in their own territories because they are fa-

A panther's home range extends over great distances and may include thick, junglelike forests as well as swamp and marshland.

miliar with the land and the habits of local prey. Territories are important for breeding as well, because the male and female panthers are aware of each other's whereabouts.

COMMUNICATING CATS

Although Florida panthers are private animals, they communicate with each other through their senses of smell, sight, touch, and sound.

Kittens make a variety of sounds, including chirps, whistles, peeps, purrs, moans, and growls. When kittens begin playing, just before a chase, they make a few low, short whistles. If they become frightened, they may make a series of short, high-pitched peeps before they run for cover. Kittens communicate with their mother by making chirping noises, and they whistle if they want their mother to know where they are. People who have raised Florida panthers in captivity report that the cats recognize the people they see regularly and greet them each with a different distinctive sound.

Florida panthers also communicate through body language. When they feel threatened, they lower their ears against their heads. If they are content, both ears stand straight up. When panthers are frustrated and confused, their ears move in different directions, and their facial expressions change constantly. When a panther is about to attack, it lowers its ears flat against its head, pulls back its lips to show its big teeth, and growls or hisses menacingly.

One of the most important ways that panthers communicate with each other is with the "scrape," which is used to mark a panther's territory. Males typically leave more scrapes than females. The panther uses his hind feet to scrape soil, leaves, and pine needles into a pile, then marks it with his scent by leaving urine on the pile. He may also mark a scrape with scent from the glands just under his tail. Each scrape is about 6 to 8 inches (15 to 20 centimeters) long.

The male panther leaves his scrapes at key points: along the boundary where his territory meets that of another male, along pathways, and in places where he has hidden food from a catch that was too large to eat all at once. The scrape is a sort of "No Trespassing" sign. Other panthers passing by sniff at the scrapes to find out who is living there and how long ago the mark was made. Often they mark the scrape with their own scent, to leave the message that they have passed by. Female panthers occasionally make scrapes too, especially during the mating season. Females with kittens do not advertise their presence, however, and often cover their feces with dirt to avoid attracting adult males, which might harm the kittens.

READY FOR MATING

Adult male panthers are sexually mature when they are about three years old. Females are ready to mate between the ages of two and three. Most breeding occurs when the male and female territories overlap. Males may mate with several females, but the female usually mates with only one male during estrus, the period in which she is ready for mating. If two males are attracted to the same female, the males may fight each other to decide who will mate with the female. In rare cases, when the territories of two males overlap, a female will mate with more than one male. Each male, however, usually mates with all the females that live in his territory, visiting each one in turn when she is in estrus.

A male can tell when a female in the area is ready to mate by the scent marks that she leaves. During estrus, she produces special chemical signals that male panthers recognize. Often a female that is ready to mate actively seeks out the male whose territory is nearby. The mating pair may stay together for as many as sixteen days and mate repeatedly during that time. Once the female's mating period ends, the male leaves her territory.

THE NEW GENERATION

Although Florida panthers can breed at any time of the year, most litters are born during late spring. The gestation period (the amount of time that the female is pregnant) is between 90 and 95 days. Females give birth in dens, which provide protection from heavy rains or hot sun. A female may give birth to as many as four kittens, although a litter of two is more typical. These kittens are born blind and helpless. The mother feeds them her milk for about two months, and then the kittens are ready to eat fresh meat.

The female panther is the sole provider for her kittens. She often leaves her kittens for long periods of time so she can hunt for food. This can be a dangerous time for kittens because they are vulnerable to predators, including adult male panthers. Adult male panthers have been known to kill and eat kittens that are as large as 50 pounds (23 kilograms). Kittens may stay with their mother for as long as two years. During this time, they follow her throughout her territory and develop the hunting skills they will need to survive on their own in the wild.

When the female is ready to mate again, she leads her kittens, who are now ready to fend for themselves, to one last kill of prey. She then leaves them there and does not return. The siblings will

stay together for a few days until they are ready to go their separate ways. The kittens then have to fend for themselves for the first time. A number of them may die during the first weeks or months of their independence—some because they are inexperienced hunters and cannot catch enough food; others because they wander into the territories of adult male panthers and are attacked or wander onto highways while looking for home ranges of their own. The young males travel the greatest distances and are more likely to cross highways than females.

ON THE BRINK OF EXTINCTION

The Florida panther has no natural enemies except for humans and other panthers. For a long time, while government agencies offered protection to game animals, other species—including cougars, as well as snakes, wolves, coyotes, bears, and poisonous plants—were considered "bad" and were eliminated. In the 1960s people began to realize the important function that cougars play in nature. Like other predators, these big cats play a vital role in the recycling of nutrients, which helps the land to support new life.

This natural system in which plants and animals find and provide food is called the food chain. Predators, like the cougar, are at the top of the food chain. When the cougar kills a deer, for example, the parts of the deer's body that the cougar eats are digested into food materials and the excess is eliminated as waste. The cougar's waste products, as well as the parts of the carcass that are left to decay, are eventually broken down by bacteria into minerals and other chemicals. These chemicals are returned to the soil, where they provide nourishment for plants, and the cycle begins again. Each member of the food chain is important in helping to maintain the balance of nature.

THE DECLINE OF THE PANTHER

The Florida panther population began to decrease as early as the 1500s, when humans first settled on its land. Until then, Florida panthers were able to roam the land freely. But as people moved into panther territory, the animals were hunted and killed. The efforts made to protect the panthers since 1958 (when the Florida panther was given legal protection by the state of Florida) angered

The Florida Everglades, a natural habitat for the Florida panther, has been disrupted by the construction of buildings and roads like Alligator Alley.

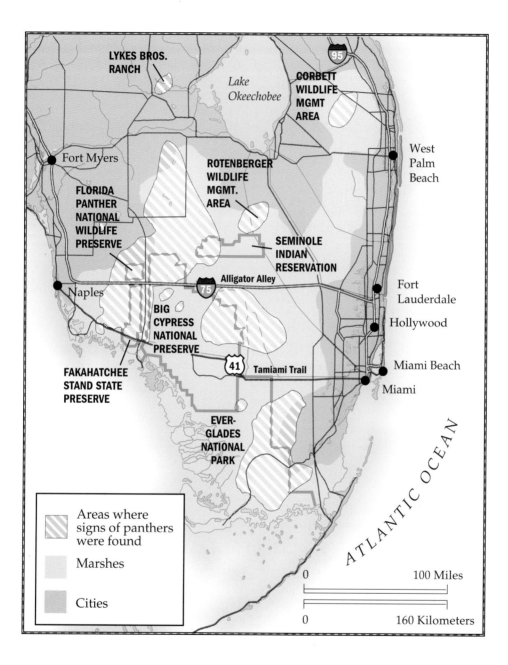

LYKES BROS. RANCH

Lake Okeechobee

CORBETT WILDLIFE MGMT AREA

Fort Myers

ROTENBERGER WILDLIFE MGMT. AREA

West Palm Beach

FLORIDA PANTHER NATIONAL WILDLIFE PRESERVE

SEMINOLE INDIAN RESERVATION

75 Alligator Alley

Naples

Fort Lauderdale

BIG CYPRESS NATIONAL PRESERVE

Hollywood

FAKAHATCHEE STAND STATE PRESERVE

41 Tamiami Trail

Miami Beach

Miami

EVER-GLADES NATIONAL PARK

ATLANTIC OCEAN

Areas where signs of panthers were found

Marshes

Cities

0   100 Miles

0   160 Kilometers

many hunters, who continued to hunt them illegally. Hunters have also threatened the panther's survival by killing deer and hogs, reducing the amount of prey available to the native predators.

One of the greatest threats to the Florida panther today is loss of habitat. Since 1960, Florida's human population has more than doubled. Originally, the Everglades covered 4 million acres (1.6 million hectares) of southeast Florida from Lake Okeechobee to the Everglades National Park. Since 1948, 2 million acres (810,000 hectares) have been drained between the lake and the park to establish farms and stimulate urban development. The construction of cities and roadways contributed to the drying of the wetlands, making it easier for people and their vehicles to penetrate wilderness lands. This "invasion" forced the panthers to leave their home range and cross dangerous, newly built highways.

In 1928 the Tamiami Trail, connecting Miami with Tampa, was completed. This was the first road built across southern Florida. In 1943, State Road 29 was built just north of Tamiami Trail, but most of Florida's wetlands were still inaccessible. Then, in the 1960s, State Road 84, known as Alligator Alley (now Interstate 75), was built across southern Florida and gave people direct access to the heart of panther territory. Within fifteen years, twenty panther deaths and six injuries resulted from highway collisions.

THREATS OF DISEASE

The introduction of civilization into panther territory creates serious health problems for the Florida panther, too. Panthers who are not able to catch enough prey are weakened and are less able to fight off disease and parasites. Panthers may develop feline distemper, a highly contagious and often fatal viral disease. The cats can catch one of the two types of distemper (feline panleukopenia and feline calcivirus) by eating prey that has been infected with the virus that causes it.

Other potentially dangerous diseases include rabies and pseudorabies. Wild hogs carry pseudorabies virus, and panthers often feed on wild hogs. There is no documented evidence that panthers die from pseudorabies, however. Although panthers tend to be scarce in areas where wild hogs are plentiful, the reason may be that people hunt in these areas and disturb the habitat.

A variety of parasites can also attack Florida panthers. One parasite, the hookworm, can be particularly devastating because it can cause severe anemia (a blood deficiency) and weight loss. It may also contribute to kitten mortality because the parasite can be transmitted through the mother's milk.

THE THREAT OF POLLUTION

Pollution is another major health concern for panthers and other wildlife species. The pesticides used in agriculture are carried by the rain into streams and rivers. The waste products created by sugar production and other industries can also contaminate the water that drains into the swamps in panther territory. In 1989 a panther that died in the Everglades had an extremely high level of mercury in her blood and tissues. She was believed to have died of mercury poisoning, which destroys brain cells and can be passed from mother to offspring in the womb, causing nerve damage in kittens. Other panthers from the southern part of that territory were also found to be carrying large amounts of mercury in their bodies. Typically, they came from areas where prey was scarce, and panthers had to eat alligators and raccoons, whose bodies concentrate the mercury residues in the fish they eat.

Recently, wildlife biologists have been finding reproductive problems among wild species in areas heavily contaminated by the man-made chemicals found in pesticides and industrial waste products. Charles Facemire, an environmental toxicologist for the U.S. Fish and Wildlife Service, believes that some of these problems may be due to the pollutants.

Most experts, however, believe that the panther's health problems are the result of inbreeding (mating between closely related animals). As the panther's range and population have become smaller and isolated, inbreeding has become common. Because fewer mates are available, offspring mate with parents, and siblings mate with each other. In small populations, certain hereditary traits may occur more often than in larger populations. Other traits may be lost, making the members of the inbred group less varied than their ancestors.

Normal hereditary variation, which scientists call genetic diversity, helps to provide greater protection against challenges such as disease. Inbreeding may have made the immune systems of Florida panthers less effective against viruses and parasites, causing a higher death rate among kittens.

The extent of inbreeding has become so great that most Florida panthers are born with one or more abnormal physical traits. The two most distinctive characteristics of today's Florida panthers—a tail with a 90-degree kink near the end and a whorl of fur (cowlick) on the panther's back—are believed to be the results of inbreeding. These traits occur occasionally in other cougar populations, but they are far more common among the Florida panthers. A kinked tail and a cowlick do not harm a panther's chances for survival, but a number of more serious changes have also occurred. Many males are born with glandular disorders that can hamper their ability to reproduce. Another serious concern is that more panthers are being born with holes in their hearts—an inherited condition. These genetic weaknesses, along with the other threats to the animal's welfare, have contributed to the steady decline of the Florida panther.

WAS THE FLORIDA PANTHER EXTINCT?

By the late 1960s the population of the Florida panther had dwindled so much that it was rare to spot a live one. Some people were convinced that the Florida panther had become extinct. In 1967 the remains of a 70-pound (32-kilogram) male were found in the Ocala National Forest. In 1969 a male panther, weighing more than 100 pounds (45 kilograms), was shot by a deputy sheriff. In 1972 a large male panther was injured by a car and later shot by a highway policeman. At the time, some people believed that these were the last of the Florida panthers. Concerned environmentalists, however, hoped there were more, and in 1972 the World Wildlife Fund hired puma hunters Roy McBride and Ronald Nowak to find them.

In 1973 a very old female panther was discovered near Fisheating Creek. This discovery was very encouraging, but no one could be certain if there were any more panthers left in the wild.

SAVING THE FLORIDA PANTHER

In March 1976, Peter C. H. Pritchard of the Florida Audubon Society held a Florida Panther Conference. He invited people who he believed knew something about the Florida panther. The information shared by these many "experts" was conflicting, however. "It became clear that no one really knew much about the panther. We didn't even know whether or not it still existed," said Chris Belden, a biologist who attended as a representative of the Florida Game and Fresh Water Fish Commission.

A few months after the conference, Chris Belden was put in charge of the Florida Panther Recovery Team in an effort to learn more about the panthers. His job was to conduct field studies and search for any animals that might still remain. For several years Belden devoted his life to trying to save the Florida panther. Belden and his team came across numerous signs of the wild cat, which included panther scrapes, prints, and scat (feces), but they did not have much luck finding an actual Florida panther.

TRACKING PANTHERS

In 1981, Belden, with a professional hunter and two trained "cat" dogs, finally located and treed (drove up a tree) a male panther in the Fakahatchee Strand. This was the first time that Belden had been in close contact with a panther. A second male panther was captured ten days later. Once they had calmed the panthers with a tranquilizing drug and got them safely to the ground, they put radio collars on them. Then they released the panthers and began tracking them.

The collaring technique, called radio telemetry, has been useful in studying the Florida panther. By tracking the panthers' movements, scientists can learn all about the animals' habits and preferences, as well as how many panthers there are and where they are. Researchers can also determine the extent of a typical panther's range, the type of land it prefers, and its hunting and mating practices. In 1983, Belden's team went on what seemed like a ordinary mission—to replace the batteries in the radio collar of a young female. The panther was treed by hounds, and the biologists shot a tranquilizer dart into her leg. The dose of the drug was the same that had been used when the panther was first collared, but this time the dart pierced an artery instead of a muscle. The entire dose of the drug entered the panther's bloodstream at once, and she died. Because of this incident, many people became critical of the radio-tracking program.

Several months later, the Game and Fresh Water Fish Commission remedied the situation by hiring veterinarian Melody Roelke, who was specially trained to work with large cats. Her job was to determine whether the panther was strong enough to tolerate a capture and be collared. If the panther appeared weak or sickly, Roelke did not attempt a capture. Her responsibilities also included providing medical care for the cats when necessary.

AN UNOFFICIAL CAPTIVE-BREEDING PROGRAM

Robert Baudy, owner of the Rare Feline Breeding Compound in rural Sumter County, was an accomplished breeder of wild cats. He had successfully bred 27 species of cats in captivity, which produced more than 2,675 offspring. In 1976, Baudy's expertise earned him a position on the Florida Panther Recovery Team.

After two years on the Recovery Team, Baudy grew impatient—there was still no sign of a captive-breeding program, which he had hoped to oversee. On June 1, 1978, he wrote a letter to the members of the Recovery Team and announced that he was going to start his own captive-breeding program. In the letter, Baudy told them that he had purchased one male and two female Florida panthers, which had been on display at the Everglades Wonder Gardens, a zoological attraction in Bonita Springs owned by Bill and Lester Piper. The Piper brothers had raised Florida panthers since 1941, when three panther kittens were brought to the Wonder Gardens. A male was added in 1945 and a female in 1958. The breeding stock of Florida panthers at the Wonder Gardens was known as the "Piper stock."

Baudy could not convince the Recovery Team of the importance of captive breeding. Even without government support, how-

Chris Belden, collaring a captured panther. The radio telemetry collar allows scientists to track the animal's movements.

How Is a Panther Captured?

WHEN TRACKS, scrapes, or other evidence of a panther are found in an area, professional hunters search the woods and swamps with their hounds. The dogs sniff out the cat and chase it up a tree. The hunters then guard the animal until a team of biologists and a veterinarian arrive.

The veterinarian decides if the panther is healthy enough to be handled. If it is, the veterinarian shoots the animal with a tranquilizer dart. After a few minutes, the panther is calm and falls down onto a large, air-filled cushion. Sometimes a biologist climbs the tree and wraps a rope around the cat's chest to lower the animal to the ground.

The veterinarian examines the panther closely, administers vitamins and vaccines for rabies and feline distemper, and collects blood, sperm, and tissue samples for medical and genetic testing. Once the tests are completed, the panther is fitted with a radio collar. For the rest of its life, the panther will be tracked and recaptured every few years to have its collar replaced.

ever, he was very successful with his unofficial captive-breeding program. Working by himself, Baudy raised more than a hundred Florida panther offspring, which were donated or sold to various animal collections.

THE BIG GUY RESCUE

In November 1984, a team of wildlife officials and veterinarians rushed to the aid of a young male Florida panther. The animal had been found on the Tamiami Trail, badly injured from a highway hit-and-run accident. By the time the panther was brought to the veterinary school hospital of the University of Florida in Gainesville, he had been nicknamed "Big Guy." After treatment and a series of operations, Big Guy was on the way to a successful recovery.

Originally, the Florida Game and Fresh Water Fish Commission planned to return Big Guy to the wild, but he was not strong enough. Big Guy remained at the commission's research lab in Gainesville while he recovered.

The rescue and recovery of Big Guy increased the interest in a captive-breeding program. Because Big Guy was already in captivity, biologists felt that he would be a perfect candidate.

Big Guy was then transferred to a captive-breeding facility called White Oak Plantation, which was on 8,000 wooded acres (3,238 hectares) in Nassau County. Biologists planned to make Big Guy the focus of the captive-breeding program. The first stage was to have Big Guy practice breeding with female Texas cougars. This experiment would help the scientists develop guidelines for breeding Florida panthers.

By 1985, Big Guy was healthy enough to participate in the preliminary breeding experiments. Unfortunately, when his keepers put three female Texas cougars in his breeding pen of three fourths of an acre (.25 hectare), Big Guy showed no interest in them. Four years later, Big Guy was put in an enclosure of 15 acres (6 hectares). As soon as he was back in a wide, open space, he turned into a wild animal again. He mated with one of the cougars, but although for a while she seemed to be pregnant, she was not.

TO BREED OR NOT TO BREED

In 1989 the U.S. Fish and Wildlife Service asked the International Union for the Conservation of Nature and Natural Resources for some advice: What would be the best way to save the Florida panther from extinction? Captive-breeding experts Ulysses Seal and Robert Lacy of the International Union used a computer program called VORTEX to analyze information about the panther population. The program predicted that without captive breeding, there was an 85 percent chance that the big cats would die out within twenty-five to forty years. Adults in the wild would have trouble finding mates, so inbreeding would increase, and valuable genes would be lost in each new generation. Even worse, a natural disaster or an outbreak of disease could wipe out the whole population at once.

VORTEX also presented a plan for panther survival. If a breeding program were set up, with 130 animals in wild and captive environments by the year 2000 and 500 by the year 2010, the Florida panther would have a 95 percent probability of surviving in the wild for the next hundred years. Ninety percent of the genes carried by the current panther population would also be preserved.

Big Guy.

THE FIRST OFFICIAL CAPTIVE BREEDING PROGRAM

In January 1990, the Fish and Wildlife Service made plans to issue the Endangered Species permits needed to begin the Captive Breeding Program. These permits would allow biologists from the Florida Game and Fresh Water Fish Commission to capture as many as six kittens and four adults in 1991 and six kittens and two adults each year for another five years. The scientists would be able to plan the mating of these animals carefully to preserve the good traits of the panthers in the offspring.

Critics of the program claimed that removing animals from the wild would disrupt the reproduction of the remaining wild populations. Florida panther coordinator Dennis Jordan explained that they would be removing mostly kittens. If the whole litter were taken, mother would go into estrus and breed again. About 50 percent of the kittens born in the wild die before they are six months old, so taking some kittens from the litter would not hurt the remaining population. Instead, the chances of survival would improve for the kittens left behind because there would be less competition.

The captive-breeding program was backed by many environmental groups, including the Defenders of Wildlife, the National Audubon Society, and the Sierra Club. Some animal-rights groups were not convinced, however. Holly Jensen, an animal-rights activist backed by the Fund for Animals, organized a protest against the program. In early 1990, the protesters threatened to sue the U.S. Fish and Wildlife Service unless it analyzed the effect that removing the kittens from the wild would have on the environment. They also claimed that the capture of adult cats would disrupt the panthers' social structure.

As the debate continued, permission to take the first kittens was postponed until January 1991. Then, just before the cats were going to be captured, Jensen and her group filed their lawsuit. The suit was quickly settled out of court. The Fish and Wildlife Service agreed to capture only kittens for the first year. The Service also agreed to focus on managing the panthers' habitat and other areas that the Fund for Animals felt needed more attention. Finally, during the early months of 1991, the first six kittens were taken into captivity at White Oak Plantation. Unfortunately, during the many months of arguing, at least eleven cats had died in the wild.

The purpose of the Captive Breeding Program was to collect kittens from unrelated families and mate them in captivity to eliminate the inbreeding problems of the Florida panther. When the panthers were returned to the wild, they would be dispersed to different areas, so that, in the case of a hurricane or a virus epidemic, not all the animals would be lost.

The Captive Breeding Program would not solve all the panthers' problems, however. Captive-bred panthers would have to be conditioned to survive in the wild, which was not an easy task.

In 1988, as a test, Chris Belden released seven radio-collared Texas cougars into an area north of the Osceola National Forest. He was experimenting to find the best strategy to use later when returning panthers to their habitat. The results were disappointing. Although the cougars had plenty of room to roam and plenty of deer to eat, they also had some trouble.

Within a month, one cougar was found floating in the Suwannee River—the cause of death unknown. Two were killed illegally by

Holly Jensen is committed to saving the panther and other animals. "There's very little time left," she said in an interview with *Florida Magazine.* "I firmly believe that we're the most important generation that ever lived."

hunters. Three cougars strayed beyond the study area—one discovered a private exotic game ranch where she killed five black buck antelopes from India; another ended up in the suburbs of Jacksonville, 50 miles (80 kilometers) away; and the other traveled to a goat farm over the Georgia border and killed several goats. These problems angered hunters and ranchers, which forced Belden to cut the program short. By the tenth month of the experiment, the last cougar left in the wild was recaptured and shipped back to Texas.

HIGH-TECH TESTS

Ten kittens were taken from the wild for the Captive Breeding Program in 1991 and 1992. In some cases all the kittens in the litter were taken; in others, the mother was left with one or more to raise herself. Just as the recovery team had hoped, the program seemed to have little effect on the wild population. The females who had been left with kittens raised them successfully. Those whose whole litter was taken for the breeding program soon mated again and raised a new litter.

Before the captive kittens were old enough to breed, however, panther experts saw disturbing signs of inbreeding, which it seemed might have already gone too far. They feared that breeding panthers from this highly inbred population would not help the situation. They wondered if they should try to restore the genetic health of the Florida panther by breeding it with the Texas cougar.

Then they discovered that nature had already been conducting an experiment along those same lines. In 1990, Melody Roelke noticed that there were two distinct population segments. The main group of panthers, about thirty to forty adults with their kittens, lived in and around the northern part of Big Cypress Swamp, ranging northward into the private cattle ranches in south-central Florida.

A smaller group of about ten panthers lived in Everglades National Park and the surrounding area. The biologists expected that the smaller population would be more inbred and in poorer general health than the larger group, but the Everglades panthers did not seem to have those problems. They did not have congential heart defects, and the males did not have reproductive difficulties. In fact, the males in the Everglades had healthier sperm than the Big Cypress panthers. They looked different, too. They were smaller, with a reddish tint to their fur, and without the typical cowlicks and kinked tails.

Melody Roelke consulted Stephen O'Brien, a genetics expert who had studied a number of wildlife species. By analyzing fragments of DNA (the chemical that carries an organism's hereditary traits) and other chemicals in the blood and tissues, genetic experts like O'Brien can trace family, race, or species. Roelke learned his lab techniques and tested blood samples she had collected from Florida panthers. She compared these to samples collected from eight subspecies of North American pumas and three South American subspecies. The tests showed that the Everglades panthers carried genes that seemed to have come from South or Central America!

How could that have happened? Florida panthers once bred freely with eastern mountain lions and Texas cougars, but their territory could not have overlapped with South or Central America.

Roelke studied the records at Everglades National Park. She discovered that from 1957 to 1965 the Pipers of the Everglades Wonder Gardens had released at least seven panthers from their animal collection into the wild. Roelke tested the blood of one of the panthers still in the Piper collection and found that that panther was also carrying some South or Central American genes. It seemed likely that the Piper stock contributed the genes that helped to strengthen the Everglades panthers.

Veterinarians Melody Roelke and Scott Citino at a panther capture.

This discovery—that some of the wild Florida panthers are hybrids, a mix of the Florida panther and another cougar subspecies—created a potential legal problem: The Endangered Species Act does not provide protection for hybrid animals. Fortunately, however, it does protect distinct population segments of wildlife, which would include the Florida panthers.

FUTURE OF THE FLORIDA PANTHER

The Florida Panther Recovery Plan was established in 1981, but the total panther population in the wild is still estimated at only thirty to fifty adult animals and an undetermined number of kittens. The start of the captive-breeding program, which was created to preserve the genetic heritage of the wild population, was unfortunately delayed. As a result, many valuable "founder" animals (those carrying genes not shared by some other members of the population) were lost. The program is now on hold, without having produced any new offspring.

Just how endangered is the Florida panther? Has any progress been made toward saving it, or will the panther soon be extinct?

PANTHER POLITICS

Several federal and state agencies, as well as a number of private organizations, are involved in efforts to save the Florida panther from extinction. The U.S. Fish and Wildlife Service is a leader in the effort, but its funds are limited and it is reluctant to intrude into state affairs. The Florida Game and Fresh Water Fish Commission is the primary agency involved in panther studies and the recovery program. The commission receives funding from the Panther Trust Fund, including revenues from the panther license-plate program. The National Park Service also plays a key role because much of the current panther territory is located in national parks—the Big Cypress National Preserve and the Everglades National Park. A number of environmentalist and animal-rights groups, as well as local grass-roots organizations, are also involved in the cause.

With so many diverse groups involved, there are differences of opinion as well as complaints about how matters are being handled. In 1993, Ken Alvarez, who served as the head of the Florida Panther Technical Advisory Council, wrote *Twilight of the Panther,* a book that details the "grim chronicle of wasted years and dollars, and dissipated energies."

The number one threat to Florida panther survival today, according to environmentalist Brian Hunt, is politics. He says that the Florida Game and Fresh Water Fish Commission has ties with landowners and recreational users of wildlife resources. He believes that these ties make it difficult for the commission to make objective decisions on policies regarding panther recovery. The National Park Service, too, tends to emphasize the needs of recreational users, such as hunters. Yet hunting puts stress on panthers in the wild by competing for deer and creates a disturbance that may interfere with the mating and raising of the young.

An even greater threat is posed by land development, which often converts native landscapes into farmland or cities and towns.

The loss of habitat is a major threat to the panther's long-term survival, but Florida land developers are politically very powerful. Nonetheless, despite all these pressures and a very slow start, efforts to help save the panther are making some progress.

RESTORING LOST GENES

The original purpose of the Captive Breeding Program was to preserve the panther genes and to breed animals that could be released into other parts of the panther's former range. The emphasis of the recovery effort has shifted to restoring the Florida panther to what it was before it became isolated and inbred.

In the spring and summer of 1995, eight Texas cougars were released into panther areas: two in the Fakahatchee Strand State Preserve, four in Big Cypress National Preserve, and two in Everglades National Park. It took a while for some of the Texas females to get used to their new surroundings, but they all eventually settled in and established home territories. They soon became acquainted with the resident males, and within a year, two of the new females had given birth to litters and were raising their kittens successfully.

This influx of new genes into the Florida population is a logical approach to strengthening the panther, says Darrell Land, a Florida Game and Freshwater Fish Commission wildlife biologist involved in the project. The program is not changing the Florida panther; it is simply linking the two subspecies again. Fifty percent of the genes of the new kittens are Florida panther genes. If they eventually mate with Florida panthers, their offspring will be 75 percent Florida panther and 25 percent Texas cougar.

Scientists may decide to remove the Texas females from the territory after the kittens become independent, to keep the dilution of Florida panther genes to a minimum. Young Florida panther males who have been unable to establish a territory because there are no vacancies in their local area may be moved into other parts of the panther range where males are scarce. Frozen samples of sperm may be used to impregnate females that would not have an opportunity to mate with "founder" animals under normal circumstances. The breeding process might even be speeded up by joining the eggs and sperm of Florida panthers in a laboratory and transferring them to female Texas cougars. The cougars would act as "surrogate mothers," bearing and raising the kittens, while the scarce Florida panther females would mate in the normal way.

LEARNING FROM MISTAKES

The areas in which Florida panthers are currently living cannot support many more than the thirty to fifty adult animals already there. So if the programs are successful in increasing their numbers, some panthers will have to be placed somewhere else. The logical choice would be those areas that made up part of the panther's range in the past—such as parts of northern Florida and Georgia.

The Florida Panther Recovery Team analyzed the results of the first attempt to release Texas cougars in northern Florida, trying to determine why the test ran into so many problems. The team concluded that the cougars were released too close to the hunting season and had not established home territories before hunting activity began. As a result, the animals strayed out of the area and got into trouble.

The state wildlife biologists learned from their mistakes and tried again. In February 1993, long before the start of hunting season, ten mountain lions (six females and four males) were fitted with radio collars and released in northern Florida. Nine more were released later. Some of the cats had been taken from the wild; others had been raised in captivity. The males had been neutered so that they would be unable to father kittens. (If the cougars were allowed to reproduce, they would establish a population of cougars in the area, which was not what the biologists intended.)

Special precautions were taken to keep the animals as wild as possible and give them the opportunity to learn survival skills. In the reintroduction studies in northern Florida, the Texas cougars were held, one or two at a time, in a 15-acre (6-hectare) conditioning pen. In preparation for their release, they ate only live prey (rabbits and small deer), which they had to catch.

Fifteen of the nineteen mountain lions established home ranges in northern Florida and southern Georgia. (Two were killed within a few months—one illegally by a hunter and the other on the highway. One had to be recaptured because of complaints by a local landowner. The last, a captive-bred kitten, would not follow her mother and was too young to survive on her own.) The females who had been wild-caught but held in captivity for years settled down most rapidly and established home ranges within a few days. The captive-raised animals established home ranges within a few weeks. The wild-caught animals traveled around for a few months

Where's Waldo?

IN MARCH 1995, turkey hunters found panther tracks near the town of Waldo, Florida. None of the radio-collared animals were in that area, but panther tracks were found twice more. Could there be a Florida panther living in the northern part of the state?

In April, biologists from the game commission's Wildlife Research Laboratory captured the cat (a male cougar). They fitted him with a radio collar and sent samples of his blood to Stephen O'Brien's genetic laboratory in Maryland. Then they returned the cougar to the place where he had been found.

Analysis of the Waldo cat's DNA and enzymes proved that he was the son of two of the Texas cougars that had been released in the program. The biologists recaptured him.

The Florida Game and Fresh Water Fish Commission spent five months looking for homes for the cougars in the program, then turned them over to an animal dealer in New Smyrna Beach. The dealer gradually found buyers for the cougars. "Waldo" was sold to a dealer in South Carolina, then sent to another dealer in Missouri, and after that, to a dealer in Texas. When the media found out, a furious controversy began. State biologists considered Waldo a part of their experiment, but animal-rights activists claimed that he had been born in the wild in Florida, and his removal was illegal.

Eventually the U.S. Fish and Wildlife Service stepped in, traced Waldo to a dealer who was about to sell him for use in a hunt, and returned him to Florida. Waldo was taken to the White Oak Plantation, where he is now living in captivity until a final decision is made.

before settling down. (One wild-caught male established three use areas and two home ranges and traveled back and forth around the circuit visiting each one in turn.)

Because animals raised in captivity settle down rapidly and have less tendency to wander, they may seem the best candidates for future reintroduction programs. But captive-raised animals get used to humans and lose their fear of people. When they are released in the wild, they do not avoid humans as the wild-born cats do, and they may even seek contact with humans. When panthers are seen too often, some people are disturbed and become angry or fearful.

During the course of the program, a small but very vocal group of people objected fiercely to the idea of reintroducing panthers into the wild. They spoke out at public meetings and wrote letters, articles, and editorials in local newspapers, playing on people's fears in an attempt to build opposition to the program. One woman even claimed that the commission intended to reintroduce the sabretooth tiger into northern Florida. (Since that species has been extinct for thousands of years, that would be quite a feat!)

In mid-1995, the Texas cougars that had been released were removed from the wild, and the biologists analyzed the results. In one way the study had been a success: It proved that, biologically, a reintroduction program could succeed. Politically and socially, however, there were strong pressures against its success. In the future, wildlife experts would have to do a better public-relations job with local residents. They would have to make people comfortable with the idea of panthers again living in the wild and reassure them that the presence of panthers will not interfere with other activities, such as hunting.

A PLACE FOR PANTHERS

For many years, the federal government and the state of Florida have been buying land in wilderness areas to preserve and protect the wildlife there. The establishment of Everglades National Park in 1947 protected part of the panther habitat. The establishment of Big Cypress National Preserve and the Fakahatchee Strand State Preserve in 1974 protected nearly 650,000 acres (263,000 hectares) more. Additional land purchases have substantially expanded these refuges.

The addition of the Florida Panther National Wildlife Refuge in 1989 added another 24,000 acres (9,700 hectares) of key panther habitat that included parts of the ranges of several panthers and linked other protected areas. After establishing the Fakahatchee Strand State Preserve, Florida later set up a program to buy $300 million worth of public lands each year for ten years. Private organizations have also helped to place wilderness areas under government protection. The Nature Conservancy, for example, purchases parcels of land and donates them to the government. As a result, nearly half of the Florida panther population lives on protected public lands.

But what about the other half? And what about the new populations of panthers yet to be established, which will need huge areas of land?

The Florida Game and Fresh Water Fish Commission is working closely with landowners, trying to convince them not to develop the wilderness areas that they own. In return, local landowners want it to be easier for them to obtain permits to develop other parts of their land, and they want some relief from income and other taxes. The commission is trying to make permits easier to get, but there is not much hope of income-tax relief (a number of bills already in Congress would lighten inheritance taxes, however).

In 1985 the Florida Panther Technical Advisory Council, headed by Ken Alvarez, recommended that the available protected areas could support a larger number of panthers if the wildlife managers planted grass and other forage to support more deer. Unfortunately, this simple and relatively inexpensive measure ran up against a basic policy of the National Park Service to try to re-create the conditions of "primitive America." Planting grass in wilderness areas was felt to be unnatural—even though the lands were already overrun by imported plants on which deer do not feed. Years later, food plots were set up to attract deer in some of the protected panther habitats, including the Fakahatchee Strand State Preserve and the Florida Panther National Wildlife Refuge.

TAKING THE LOW ROAD

Another promising program has greatly reduced the number of panthers and other wildlife that are killed on the highways. Automobile or truck collisions are among the main causes of death of Florida panthers. When Alligator Alley, which used to be a notorious death trap for animals, was converted from a state road to Interstate 75, the new highway design incorporated a number of

Preserving the wetland wilderness is important to the Florida panther's survival—and to the survival of the human population, too.

wildlife crossings. Ground-level underpasses consisting of two parallel walkways, each 8 feet (2.5 meters) high, 100 feet (30.5 meters) wide, and 175 feet (53 meters) long, allow animals to cross under the busy road safely. Fencing 10 feet (3 meters) high was installed in areas that had no underpasses, to direct the animals toward the safe crossings.

These walkways were an immediate success. Panthers, bears, deer, and other animals began to use them even while construction was going on. Panthers are no longer killed on Alligator Alley. Similar wildlife crossings have been installed on other highways, with the same rate of success.

WHY SAVE THE FLORIDA PANTHER?

Why such a big fuss about the Florida panther? If it's just another kind of mountain lion—and there are plenty of mountain lions in other parts of the country that are not endangered—why are so many people investing so much time and money to save it?

One reason is that, as environmentalist Judy Hancock puts it, "panthers are incredibly beautiful." Even more than that, however, Florida panthers are a fitting symbol for the wetland wilderness and its value to humanity. Because these animals roam so widely across the lands, searching for food and mates, wildlife biologists call them a "landscape species."

They are also regarded as an "umbrella species," because efforts to preserve their habitat will also help to save numerous other threatened species. Researchers are just beginning to learn about

Adopt a Panther

EARLY IN 1993, Walt McCown, a biologist with the panther reintroduction program, went out on a few trips with Steve Williams, a canoe outfitter and guide in White Springs, Florida. When Williams heard about the Texas cougars that would be roaming the nearby Osceola Forest, he decided to write an article in the local paper, to prepare the people in the area. He never did, though, and felt very guilty some months later, when an angry deer hunter, who had been followed by a cougar, complained until the cougar was removed.

Williams, who had studied environmental sciences in college, then wrote a series of eight articles that appeared in the sports section of the local newspaper during hunting season. He also founded the Florida Panther Society, a grass-roots organization aimed at bringing the reintroduction program to the public's attention and making people more sensitive to the environment. The society's members write to legislators, attend public meetings, and give educational programs in schools.

One of the Florida Panther Society's most successful ideas was the "Adopt a Panther" program. People who subscribed to it received a picture of "their" cat and regular updates on where it was living and what it was doing. Even some hunt clubs joined the program. During the reintroduction study, the "panthers" in the program were actually Texas cougars. After the study ended, subscribers were given pictures and information on radio-collared Florida panthers in the southern part of the state.

the important role the wetlands play in preserving the water supply and other resources on which Florida's human inhabitants depend. People did not always value this wilderness. The government provided incentives for draining swamplands rather than preserving them. In recent years, however, people have become more aware of their environment and sensitive to its needs.

A statewide telephone survey in 1995, for example, found that 91 percent of the public supported the efforts to save the Florida panther from extinction. In a local poll in the northern Florida counties directly affected by the reintroduction study, support was about 81 percent. When asked if they would support the reintroduction of panthers in their own or nearby counties, 77 percent of the people in the statewide poll said yes. In the study areas, there was a 73 percent positive response.

Will the panther thrive in the Florida wilderness? Most wildlife experts are cautious but optimistic about the next twenty-five or thirty years. The panther's chances for long-term survival as a wilderness animal depend on how much wilderness can be preserved. Saving the panther will take a tremendous effort, but many people believe the effort is worthwhile. As Steve Williams puts it, "If you kill nature, kill the earth, you kill the spirit—and you've killed yourself."

FINGERTIP FACTS

Length	Adult males are about seven feet (2 meters) from nose to tip of tail. Female panthers are about six feet (1.8 meters) or less in length.
Weight	Adult males weigh an average of 120 pounds (54 kilograms). Female panthers weigh an average of 80 pounds (36 kilograms).
Color	Yellowish-brown along the back and lighter in color on the lower chest, belly, and inner legs. The tip of the tail, back of the ears, and parts of the face are highlighted with dark brown or black. Kittens are born with spots, which disappear before the animals are two years old.
Food	Primarily white-tailed deer and wild hogs; also raccoons, armadillos, rabbits, cotton rats, birds, and insects.
Reproduction	Females are ready to breed between the ages of two and three. Most males are ready to breed at age three. Females typically give birth every other spring. Usually two kittens in a litter, but can be as many as four.
Care for young	Female takes full responsibility for her kittens; she nurses them and feeds them; she also teaches them how to hunt. Male takes no part in raising the young.

Range	Restricted to the southern part of Florida, primarily in the Big Cypress and Everglades areas.
Population	Highly threatened. An estimated 30 to 50 adult Florida panthers remain in the wild.
Social behavior	Solitary animals except during the mating season and when they are kittens and dependent on the mother.
Life span	About 12 years in the wild.

FURTHER READING

Books

Alvarez, Ken. *Twilight of the Panther.* Sarasota, FL: Myakka River Publishing, 1993.

Clark, Margaret Goff. *The Endangered Florida Panther.* New York: Cobble Hill Books, 1993.

DeBlieu, Jan. "The Panther Versus Florida," *Meant to Be Wild.* Golden, CO: Fulcrum Publishing, 1991.

Fergus, Charles. *Swamp Screamer.* New York: North Point Press/Farrar, Straus and Giroux, 1996.

Articles

Belden, Chris, "If You See a Panther," *Florida Wildlife,* September-October 1977, pp. 31-34.

Bolgiano, Chris, "Of Panthers & Prejudice," *Buzzworm,* May/June 1991, pp. 47-51.

Dold, Catherine, "Florida Panthers Get Some Outside Genes," *New York Times,* June 20, 1995, pp. C1, C4.

Fergus, Charles, "The Florida Panther Verges on Extinction," *Science,* March 8, 1991, pp. 1178-1180.

Greene, Juanita, "Panthers at the Vanishing Point," *National Parks,* July/August 1985, pp. 18-23.

Maehr, David S., E. Darrell Land, and Jayde C. Roof, "Florida Panthers," *National Geographic Research & Exploration,* Autumn 1991, pp. 414-431.

Osofsky, Steven A., "Panther Diary," *Natural History,* April 1988, pp. 50-54.

Radetsky, Peter, "Cat Fight," *Discover,* July 1992, pp. 56-63.

Internet Resources

http://cpuserver.dc.enews.com/cgi-bin/mfs/01/e/archive/1994 090194.8.html?12#mfs (Reprint of an article by Sally Deneen, "South Florida is the Last Refuge for a Big Cat Threatened by Hunters and Too Much Human Encroachment," from the September/October issue of *E/The Environmental Magazine*)

http://florida-keys.fl.us/apanther.gif (Portrait of a mother panther and her two kittens)

http://www.cathouse-fcc.org/catsinfo.html (Information about 36 species of wild cats)

http://www.envirolink.org/arrs/cougars.html ("Texas Cougars Cause Trouble in Florida")

http://www.envirolink.org/arrs/panther_cousins.html ("Florida Panthers' Fate Rides on Cougar Cousins," news release from Florida Game and Fresh Water Fish Commission, March 30, 1995)

http://www.fsw.gov/~pullen1/wildlaw/florid.html (Florida State Wildlife Policy)

http://www.math.utk.edu/~luh/panther.html (Photo and brief summary of Florida panther information)

ORGANIZATIONS

Big Cypress National Preserve
HCR 61 Box 110
Ochopee, FL 34141
(941) 695-2000

Everglades National Park
P.O. Box 279
Homestead, FL 33030
(305) 247-6211

Florida Advisory Council on Environmental Education
Room 237 Holland Building
Tallahassee, FL 32399-1400
(904) 487-0123

Florida Game and Fresh Water Fish Commission
620 South Meridian Street
Tallahassee, FL 32399

Florida Panther National Wildlife Refuge
P.O. Box 158
Naples, FL 33939
(941) 472-1100

"Adopt a Panther" Program
Florida Panther Society, Inc.
Route 1, Box 1895
White Springs, FL 32096
(904) 397-2945

Dennis Jordan
Florida Panther Coordinator
U.S. Fish and Wildlife Service
117 Newins-Ziegler Hall
University of Florida
P.O. Box 110450
Gainesville, FL 32611-0450
(352) 846-0546

White Oak Plantation
726 Ownes Road
Yulee, FL 32097
(904) 225-3200

INDEX

Page numbers in *italics*
refer to illustrations.

"Adopt a Panther" program, 55
Alligator Alley, *24*, 26, 52, 54
Alvarez, Ken, 45, 52
Animal-rights groups, 38–39, 49
Audubon Society, 8, 30, 38

Bangs, Outram, 10
Baudy, Robert, 32, 34
Belden, Chris, 30–31, *33*, 39, 41
Big Cypress National Preserve, 9, 45, 51
Big Guy, 35–36, *37*
Bobcats, 16
Body structure, 11, *15*

Captive-breeding program, 8, 32, 34–36, 38–41, 44, 46–48, 50
Citino, Scott, *43*
Claws, 13, 16
Coloration, 11

Communication, 19–20
Cory, Charles B., 10
Cougars, 10–11, 23, 39–41, 46–50, 55
Cowlick, 12, 28, 29, 42

Deer, 6, 11, 13, 14, 23, 26, 45
Defenders of Wildlife, 38

Endangered Species Act of 1973, 8, 43
Estrus, 20, 38
Everglades National Park, 26, 42, 45, 51
Extinction, 6, 8, 29
Eyes, 13–14

Facemire, Charles, 28
Fakahatchee Strand State Preserve, 51, 52
Felidae, 9
Florida Game and Fresh Water Fish Commission, 7, 30, 35, 38, 45, 49, 51

Florida Panther National Wildlife Refuge, 51, 52
Florida Panther Recovery Team, 30–32, 44, 47–48
Florida Panther Society, 55
Florida Panther Technical Advisory Council, 45, 52
Food, 6, 13, 14, 26
Footprints, 16
Fund for Animals, 38, 39

Habitats, 8, 14, 17–18, 26, 46
Hancock, Judy, 54
Highway accidents, 26, 35, 52, 54
Home ranges, 17, *18*, 48
Hunt, Brian, 45
Hunting, 6–8, 25–26, 45

Inbreeding, 28–29, 41–42

Jaguars, 9, 10
Jensen, Holly, 38, *40*
Jordan, Dennis, 38

Kittens, 11, *12*, 19–22, 22, 27, 28, 38, 39, 41, 47

Lacy, Robert, 36
Land, Darrell, 46
Leopards, 9, 10
License plates, 5, 7

Mating, 17, 18, 20–21
McBride, Roy, 29
McCown, Walt, 55

Mercury poisoning, 27–28
Mountain lions, 10, 54

National Park Service, 45, 52
Nature Conservancy, 51
Nowak, Ronald, 29

O'Brien, Stephen, 42

Panther Trust Fund, 45
Pesticides, 27, 28
Piper brothers, 32, 42
Pollution, 27–28
Pritchard, Peter C.H., 30

Radio telemetry, 31, *33*, 34
Roelke, Melody, 31–32, 41, 42, *43*

Scrapes, 19–20
Seal, Ulysses, 36
Sierra Club, 38
Speed, 13

Tail, kinked, 12, 28, 29, 42
Tamiami Trail, 26, 35
Teeth, 13
Toes, 13

U.S. Fish and Wildlife Service, 8, 36, 38, 39, 45, 49

Waldo, 49
White Oak Plantation, 35, 39, 49
Wild hogs, 13, 26, 27
Williams, Steve, 55, 56
World Wildlife Fund, 29